US Startup for Non-US Citizens

DINESH B RAUT

ISBN: 1539739252
ISBN-13: 978-1539739258

DEDICATION

To all American Startups, and New Business, I hope this book will helpful to them.

CONTENTS

ACKNOWLEDGMENTS

This book is designed to provide accurate and authoritative information in regard to the subject matter covered. It is sold with the understanding that the publisher is not engaged in rendering legal, accounting, or other professional service. No Claim is made to government works

1 INTRODUCTION

In America, failure is often seen as a natural stepping stone on the road to success. People may go to school to study one thing, take a job doing another, and then move around between companies and industries throughout their careers. The U.S. seems to celebrate comebacks as much as initial success. That's not how I experienced failure growing up in India. In India, failure is frowned upon in every instance. When I failed a few times in my early education, the sense I got – and had to fight against – was that failure was the end of the road, not a bump in the road. This tendency has no doubt led to the demise of many promising careers for countless entrepreneurs – and perhaps stopped many from even daring to try in the first place.

In the U.S., startups can secure funding on the basis of a strong concept, often without revenue or a set business model. Companies have the opportunity to prove their value proposition and test products extensively before releasing them to market.

In the U.S., where competition for talent is often fierce, startups aim to recruit the best employees by offering perks and providing a great company culture. I've also experienced how the entrepreneurial spirit is widely valued for employees within the American startup culture, perhaps first famously embodied by Google GOOGL +1.44%, which used "20% time" to encourage employees to pursue side projects in innovation.

Businesses in the U.S. are renowned for creating a great customer experience – the idea being that loyalty and repeat business is cheaper than acquiring new clientele. India is also known for customer service, but in a different way: employees of outsourced call centers, often trained to implement standards prescribed by companies from other nations. When it comes to startups, however, Indian companies aren't prioritizing how to delight customers and improve retention rates in the same way as their American counterparts.

.

2 CHOOSE YOUR BUSINESS STRUCTURE

Corporation (C Corporation)

A corporation (sometimes referred to as a C corporation) is an independent legal entity owned by shareholders. This means that the corporation itself, not the shareholders that own it, is held legally liable for the actions and debts the business incurs.

Corporations are more complex than other business structures because they tend to have costly administrative fees and complex tax and legal requirements. Because of these issues, corporations are generally suggested for established, larger companies with multiple employees.

For businesses in that position, corporations offer the ability to sell ownership shares in the business through stock offerings. "Going public" through an initial public offering (IPO) is a major selling point in attracting investment capital and high quality employees.

Forming a Corporation

A corporation is formed under the laws of the state in which it is registered. To form a corporation you'll need to establish your business name and register your legal name with your state government. If you choose to operate under a name different than the officially registered name, you'll most likely have to file a fictitious name (also known as an assumed name, trade name, or DBA name, short for "doing business as"). State

3

laws vary, but generally corporations must include a corporate designation (Corporation, Incorporated, Limited) at the end of the business name.

To register your business as a corporation, you need to file certain documents, typically articles of incorporation, with your state's Secretary of State office. Some states require corporations to establish directors and issue stock certificates to initial shareholders in the registration process. Contact your state business entity registration office to find out about specific filing requirements in the state where you form your business.

Once your business is registered, you must obtain business licenses and permits. Regulations vary by industry, state and locality. Use our Licensing & Permits tool to find a listing of federal, state and local permits, licenses and registrations you'll need to run a business.

If you are hiring employees, read more about federal and state regulations for employers.

Corporation Taxes

Corporations are required to pay federal, state, and in some cases, local taxes. Most businesses must register with the IRS and state and local revenue agencies, and receive a tax ID number or permit.

When you form a corporation, you create a separate tax-paying entity. Regular corporations are called "C corporations" because Subchapter C of Chapter 1 of the Internal Revenue Code is where you find general tax rules affecting corporations and their shareholders.

Unlike sole proprietors and partnerships, corporations pay income tax on their profits. In some cases, corporations are taxed twice - first, when the company makes a profit, and again when dividends are paid to shareholders on their personal tax returns. Corporations use IRS Form 1120 or 1120-A, U.S. Corporation Income Tax Return to report revenue to the federal government.

Shareholders who are also employees pay income tax on their wages. The corporation and the employee each pay one half of the Social Security and Medicare taxes, but this is usually a deductible business expense.

Read more about tax requirements for Corporations on IRS.gov.

Advantages of a Corporation

- *Limited Liability.* When it comes to taking responsibility for business debts and actions of a corporation, shareholders' personal assets are protected. Shareholders can generally only be held accountable for their investment in stock of the company.

- *Ability to Generate Capital.* Corporations have an advantage when it comes to raising capital for their business - the ability to raise funds through the sale of stock.

- *Corporate Tax Treatment.* Corporations file taxes separately from their owners. Owners of a corporation only pay taxes on corporate profits paid to them in the form of salaries, bonuses, and dividends, while any additional profits are awarded a corporate tax rate, which is usually lower than a personal income tax rate.

- *Attractive to Potential Employees.* Corporations are generally able to attract and hire high-quality and motivated employees because they offer competitive benefits and the potential for partial ownership through stock options.

Disadvantages of a Corporation

- *Time and Money.* Corporations are costly and time-consuming ventures to start and operate. Incorporating requires start-up, operating and tax costs that most other structures do not require.

- *Double Taxing.* In some cases, corporations are taxed twice - first, when the company makes a profit, and again when dividends are paid to shareholders.

- *Additional Paperwork.* Because corporations are highly regulated by federal, state, and in some cases local agencies, there are increased paperwork and recordkeeping burdens associated with this entity.

Limited Liability Company

A limited liability company is a hybrid type of legal structure that provides the limited liability features of a corporation and the tax efficiencies and operational flexibility of a partnership.

The "owners" of an LLC are referred to as "members" Depending on the state, the members can consist of a single individual (one owner), two or more individuals, corporations or other LLCs.

Unlike shareholders in a corporation, LLCs are not taxed as a separate business entity. Instead, all profits and losses are "passed through" the business to each member of the LLC. LLC members report profits and losses on their personal federal tax returns, just like the owners of a partnership would.

Forming an LLC

While each state has slight variations to forming an LLC, they all adhere to some general principles:

Choose a Business Name.

There are 3 rules that your LLC name needs to follow:

(1) it must be different from an existing LLC in your state,

(2) it must indicate that its an LLC (such as "LLC" or Limited Company and

(3) it must not include words restricted by your state (such as "bank" and "insurance" Your business name is automatically registered with your state when you register your business, so you do not have to go through a separate process.

Read more here about choosing a business name.

File the Articles of Organization.

The "articles of organization" is a simple document that legitimizes your LLC and includes information like your business name, address, and the names of its members. For most states, you file with the Secretary of State. However, other states may require that you file with a different office such as the State Corporation Commission, Department of Commerce and Consumer Affairs, Department of Consumer and Regulatory Affairs, or the Division of Corporations & Commercial Code. Note: there may be an associated filing fee.

Create an Operating Agreement.

Most states do not require operating agreements. However, an operating agreement is highly recommended for multi-member LLCs because it structures your LLC's finances and organization, and provides rules and regulations for smooth operation. The operating agreement usually includes percentage of interests, allocation of profits and losses, member's rights and responsibilities and other provisions.

Obtain Licenses and Permits.

Once your business is registered, you must obtain business licenses and permits. Regulations vary by industry, state and locality. Use the Licensing & Permits tool to find a listing of federal, state and local permits, licenses and registrations you'll need to run a business.

Hiring Employees.

If you are hiring employees, read more about federal and state regulations for employers.

Announce Your Business.

Some states, including Arizona and New York, require the extra step of publishing a statement in your local newspaper about your LLC formation. Check with your state's business filing office for requirements in your area.

LLC Taxes

In the eyes of the federal government, an LLC is not a separate tax entity, so the business itself is not taxed. Instead, all federal income taxes are passed on to the LLC's members and are paid through their personal income tax. While the federal government does not tax income on an LLC, some states do, so check with your state's income tax agency.

Since the federal government does not recognize LLC as a business entity for taxation purposes, all LLCs must file as a corporation, partnership, or sole proprietorship tax return. Certain LLCs are automatically classified and taxed as a corporation by federal tax law. For guidelines about how to classify an LLC, visit IRS.gov.

LLCs that are not automatically classified as a corporation can choose their business entity classification. To elect a classification, an LLC must file Form 8832. This form is also used if an LLC wishes to change its classification status.

Read more about filing as a corporation or partnership and filing as a single member LLC at IRS.gov.

You should file the following tax forms depending on your classification:

- Single Member LLC. A single-member LLC files Form 1040 Schedule C like a sole proprietor.

- Partners in an LLC. Partners in an LLC file a Form 1065 partnership tax return like owners in a traditional partnership.

- LLC filing as a Corporation. An LLC designated as a corporation files Form 1120, the corporation income tax return.

The IRS guide to Limited Liability Companies provides all relevant tax forms and additional information regarding their purpose and use.

Combining the Benefits of an LLC with an S-Corp

There is always the possibility of requesting S-Corp status for your LLC. An attorney can advise you on the pros and cons. You'll have to make a special election with the IRS to have the LLC taxed as an S-Corp using Form 2553.

You must file prior to the first two months and fifteen days of the beginning of the tax year in which the election is to take effect. For more information about S-Corp status, visit IRS.gov.

The LLC remains a limited liability company from a legal standpoint, but for tax purposes it can be treated as an S- Corp. Be sure to contact the state's income tax agency where you plan to file your election form. Ask about the tax requirements and if they recognize elections of other entities (such as the S-Corp).

Advantages of an LLC

- *Limited Liability*. Members are protected from personal liability for business decisions or actions of the LLC. This means that if the LLC incurs debt or issued, members; personal assets are usually exempt. This is similar to the liability protections afforded to shareholders of a corporation. Keep in mind that limited liability means "limited" liability - members are not necessarily shielded from wrongful acts, including those of their employees.

- *Less Recordkeeping*. An LLC's operational ease is one of its greatest advantages. Compared to an S- Corporation, there is less registration paperwork and there are smaller start-up costs.

- *Sharing of Profits*. There are fewer restrictions on profit sharing within an LLC, as members distribute profits as they see fit. Members might contribute different proportions of capital and sweat equity. Consequently, it's up to the members themselves to decide who has earned what percentage of the profits or losses.

Disadvantages of an LLC

- *Limited Life.* In many states, when a member leaves an LLC, the business is dissolved and the members must fulfill all remaining legal and business obligations to close the business. The remaining members can decide if they want to start a new LLC or part ways. However, you can include provisions in your operating agreement to prolong the life of the LLC if a member decides to leave the business.

- *Self-Employment Taxes.* Members of an LLC are considered self-employed and must pay the self- employment tax contributions towards Medicare and Social Security. The entire net income of the LLC is subject to this tax.

Partnership

A partnership is a single business where two or more people share ownership.

Each partner contributes to all aspects of the business, including money, property, labor or skill. In return, each partner shares in the profits and losses of the business.

Because partnerships entail more than one person in the decision-making process, it's important to discuss a wide variety of issues up front and develop a legal partnership agreement. This agreement should document how future business decisions will be made, including how the partners will divide profits, resolve disputes, change ownership (bring in new partners or buy out current partners) and how to dissolve the partnership. Although partnership agreements are not legally required, they are strongly recommended and it is considered extremely risky to operate without one.

Types of Partnerships

There are three general types of partnership arrangements:

- **General Partnerships** assume that profits, liability and management duties are divided equally among partners. If you opt for an unequal distribution, the percentages assigned to each partner must be documented in the partnership agreement.

- **Limited Partnerships** (also known as a partnership with limited liability) are more complex than general partnerships. Limited partnerships allow partners to have limited liability as well as limited input with management decisions. These limits depend on the extent of each partner's investment percentage. Limited partnerships are attractive to investors of short-term projects.

- **Joint Ventures** act as general partnership, but for only a limited period of time or for a single project. Partners in a joint venture can be recognized as an ongoing partnership if they continue the venture, but they must file as such.

Forming a Partnership

To form a partnership, you must register your business with your state, a process generally done through your Secretary of State's office.

You'll also need to establish your business name. For partnerships, your legal name is the name given in your partnership agreement or the last names of the partners. If you choose to operate under a name different than the officially registered name, you will most likely have to file a fictitious name (also known as an assumed name, trade name, or DBA name, short for "doing business as").

Once your business is registered, you must obtain business licenses and permits. Regulations vary by industry, state and locality. Use our Licensing & Permits tool to find a listing of federal, state and local permits, licenses and registrations you'll need to run a business.

If you are hiring employees, read more about federal and state regulations for employers.

Partnership Taxes

Most businesses will need to register with the IRS, register with state and local revenue agencies, and obtain a tax ID number or permit.

A partnership must file an "annual information return" to report the income, deductions, gains and losses from the business's operations, but the business itself does not pay income tax. Instead, the business "passes through" any profits or losses to its partners. Partners include their respective share of the partnership's income or loss on their personal tax returns.

Partnership taxes generally include:

- Annual Return of Income
- Employment Taxes
- Excise Taxes

Partners in the partnership are responsible for several additional taxes, including:

- Income Tax
- Self-Employment Tax
- Estimated Tax

Filing information for partnerships:

- Partnerships must furnish copies of their Schedule K-1 (Form 1065) to all partners by the date Form 1065 is required to be filed, including extensions.
- Partners are not employees and should not be issued a Form W-2.

The IRS guide to Partnerships provides all relevant tax forms and additional information regarding their purpose and use.

Advantages of a Partnership

- *Easy and Inexpensive.* Partnerships are generally an inexpensive and easily formed business structure. The majority of time spent starting a partnership often focuses on developing the partnership agreement.
- *Shared Financial Commitment.* In a partnership, each partner is equally invested in the success of the business. Partnerships have the advantage of pooling resources to obtain capital. This could be beneficial in terms of securing credit, or by simply doubling your seed money.
- *Complementary Skills.* A good partnership should reap the benefits of being able to utilize the strengths, resources and expertise of each partner.
- *Partnership Incentives for Employees.* Partnerships have an employment advantage over other entities if they offer employees the opportunity to become a partner. Partnership incentives often attract highly motivated and qualified employees.

Disadvantages of a Partnership

- *Joint and Individual Liability*. Similar to sole proprietorships, partnerships retain full, shared liability among the owners. Partners are not only liable for their own actions, but also for the business debts and decisions made by other partners. In addition, the personal assets of all partners can be used to satisfy the partnership's debt.
- *Disagreements Among Partners*. With multiple partners, there are bound to be disagreements Partners should consult each other on all decisions, make compromises, and resolve disputes as amicably as possible.
- *Shared Profits*. Because partnerships are jointly owned, each partner must share the successes and profits of their business with the other partners. An unequal contribution of time, effort, or resources can cause discord among partners.

Sole Proprietorship

A sole proprietorship is the simplest and most common structure chosen to start a business. It is an unincorporated business owned and run by one individual with no distinction between the business and you, the owner. You are entitled to all profits and are responsible for all your business's debts, losses and liabilities.

Forming a Sole Proprietorship

You do not have to take any formal action to form a sole proprietorship. As long as you are the only owner, this status automatically comes from your business activities. In fact, you may already own one without knowing it. If you are a freelance writer, for example, you are a sole proprietor.

But like all businesses, you need to obtain the necessary licenses and permits. Regulations vary by industry, state and locality. Use the **Licensing & Permits tool** to find a listing of federal, state and local permits, licenses and registrations you'll need to run a business.

If you choose to operate under a name different than your own, you will most likely have to file a **fictitious name** (also known as an assumed name, trade name, or DBA name, short for "doing business as"). You must choose an original name; it cannot already be claimed by another business.

Sole Proprietor Taxes

Because you and your business are one and the same, the business itself is not taxed separately-the sole proprietorship income is your income. You report income and/or losses and expenses with a **Schedule C** and the standard **Form 1040**. The "bottom-line amount" from Schedule C transfers to your personal tax return. It's your responsibility to withhold and pay all income taxes, including self-employment and estimated taxes. You can find more information about sole proprietorship taxes and **other forms** at IRS.gov.

Advantages of a Sole Proprietorship

- *Easy and inexpensive to form:* A sole proprietorship is the simplest and least expensive business structure to establish. Costs are minimal, with legal costs limited to obtaining the necessary license or permits.
- *Complete control.* Because you are the sole owner of the business, you have complete control over all decisions. You aren't required to consult with anyone else when you need to make decisions or want to make changes.
- *Easy tax preparation.* Your business is not taxed separately, so it's easy to fulfill the tax reporting requirements for a sole proprietorship. The tax rates are also the lowest of the business structures.

Disadvantages of a Proprietorship

- *Unlimited personal liability.* Because there is no legal separation between you and your business, you can be held personally liable for the debts and obligations of the business. This risk extends to any liabilities incurred as a result of employee actions.
- *Hard to raise money.* Sole proprietors often face challenges when trying to raise money. Because you can't sell stock in the business, investors won't often invest. Banks are also hesitant to lend to a sole proprietorship because of a perceived lack of credibility when it comes to repayment if the business fails.
- *Heavy burden.* The flipside of complete control is the burden and pressure it can impose. You alone are ultimately responsible for the successes and failures of your business.

3 REGISTRATION

Choose Your Business Name

Choosing a business name is an important step in the business planning process. Not only should you pick a name that reflects your brand identity, but you also need to ensure it is properly registered and protected for the long term. You should also give a thought to whether it's web-ready. Is the domain name even available?

Here are some tips to help you pick, register, and protect your business name.

Factors to Consider When Naming Your Business

Many businesses start out as freelancers, solo operations, or partnerships. In these cases, it's easy to fall back on your own name as your business name. While there's nothing wrong with this, it does make it tougher to present a professional image and build brand awareness.

Here are some points to consider as you choose a name:

- **How will your name look?** – On the web, as part of a logo, on social media.
- **What connotations does it evoke?** – Is your name too corporate or not corporate enough? Does it reflect your business philosophy and culture? Does it appeal to your market?

- **Is it unique?** – Pick a name that hasn't been claimed by others, online or offline. A quick web search and domain name search (more on this below) will alert you to any existing use.

Check for Trademarks

Trademark infringement can carry a high cost for your business. Before you pick a name, use the U.S. Patent and Trademark Office's trademark search tool to see if a similar name, or variations of it, is trademarked.

If You Intend to Incorporate

If you intend to incorporate your business, you'll need to contact your state filing office to check whether your intended business name has already been claimed and is in use. If you find a business operating under your proposed name, you may still be able to use it, provided your business and the existing business offer different goods/services or are located in different regions.

Pick a Name That is Web-Ready

In order to claim a website address or URL, your business name needs to be unique and available. It should also be rich in key words that reflect what your business does. To find out if your business name has been claimed online, do a simple web search to see if anyone is already using that name.

Next, check whether a domain name (or web address) is available. You can do this using the WHOIS database of domain names. If it is available, be sure to claim it right away. This guide explains how to register a domain name.

Claim Your Social Media Identity

It's a good idea to claim your social media name early in the naming process – even if you are not sure which sites you intend to use. A name for your Facebook page can be set up and changed, but you can only claim a vanity URL or custom URL once you've got 25 fans or "likes." This custom URL name must be unique, or un-claimed.

Register Your New Business Name

Registering a business name is a confusing area for new business owners. What does it mean and what are you required to do?

Registering your business name involves a process known as registering a "Doing Business As (DBA)" name or trade name. This process shouldn't be confused with incorporation and it doesn't provide trademark protection. Registering your "Doing Business As" name is simply the process of letting your state government know that you are doing business as a name other than your personal name or the legal name of your partnership or corporation. If you are operating under your own name, then you can skip the process.

Learn about the requirements in your state and how to file in this Registering Your Doing Business As Name guide.

Apply for Trademark Protection

A trademark protects words, names, symbols, and logos that distinguish goods and services. Your name is one of your most valuable business assets, so it's worth protecting. You can file for a trademark for less than $300. Learn how to trademark your business name.

State Authority :

If you establish your business as a sole proprietorship, you won't need to register your business at the state level. However, many states require sole proprietors to use their own name for the business name unless they formally file another name. This is known as a your Doing Business As (DBA) name, trade name or a fictitious name.

Incorporating, making the leap from a personally-owned business to one with investors, is no small decision. Corporate laws and corporate tax laws vary between states (and countries for that matter). Let's look at some of the top places to incorporate in the United States.

The Cheapest State To Do Business In

Corporate taxes are important, but they're not the only costs a business faces. If you plan on actually working where you incorporate, then the priorities shift. Forbes did a handy ranking of labor, energy and tax costs for businesses. :

1. South Dakota
2. Wyoming
3. North Carolina
4. West Virginia
5. Delaware

Quality of the Workforce

If your business is specialized, you'll probably want an educated labor force to pull from. According to the Forbes list, the top states for an educated work force are:

1. Colorado
2. Washington
3. Virginia
4. Utah
5. New Hampshire

The Economic Question

If you're looking for a state with a strong economy, Forbes ranks the top five as:

1. Texas
2. Nevada
3. Washington
4. Oklahoma
5. Colorado

But if it's projected economic growth you're after, the picture changes quite a bit:

1. Washington
2. Colorado
3. Texas
4. North Dakota
5. New Hampshire

4 OBTAIN AN EMPLOYER IDENTIFICATION NUMBER AND FILLING TAX

When starting a business, you must decide what form of business entity to establish. Your form of business (e.g., sole proprietorship, partnership, LLC) determines which income tax return form you have to file. The federal government levies four basic types of business taxes:

Federal Tax

Income tax
Self-employment tax
Taxes for employers
Excise taxes
To learn more about these taxes, visit the Internal Revenue Service's (IRS)

State Tax

In addition to business taxes required by the federal government, you will have to pay some state and local taxes. Each state and locality has its own tax laws. The links below provide access to key resources that will help you learn about your state tax obligations. Having knowledge of your state tax requirement can help you avoid problems and your business save money. The most common types of tax requirements for small business are income taxes and employment taxes.

Income Taxes

Nearly every state levies a business or corporate income tax. Your tax requirement depends on the legal structure of your business. For example, if your business is a Limited Liability Company (LLC), the LLC gets taxed separately from the owners, while sole proprietors report their personal and business income taxes using the same form. Consult the General Tax Information link under your state for specific requirements.

Employment Taxes

In addition to federal employment taxes, business owners with employees are also responsible for paying certain taxes required by the state. All states require payment of state workers' compensation insurance and unemployment insurance taxes.

The following states/territories also require a business to pay for temporary disability insurance:

1.   California
2.   Hawaii
3.   New Jersey
4.   New York
5.   Rhode Island
6.   Puerto Rico

5 BANK ACCOUNT

Opening a business bank account online can be an easy and painless process when you have all the necessary documentation in place.

First, it is important to realize there are several factors that can prohibit one from opening a business bank account on the internet.

For example, if a company provides money services, including check cashing, issuing money orders, issuing store value cards, exchanging currency, or wiring funds in exchange for a fee, banks will not allow you to open an account online. You will need to go to the branch personally to open an account.

In addition, if your business is in one of the following industries, then you will need to open an account in person rather than online.

- Telemarketing
- Precious metal dealers
- Gambling
- Government entities

So, what type of documentation is required to open a business bank account online? Depending on the structure of your business, the following documents will be required to open an account online.

Sole Proprietorship

Social Security Number or Business Tax Identification Number

- Business License showing both business and owner's name, or
- Business name filing document, such as a Fictitious Name Certificate or Certificate of Trade Name, showing both business and owner's name

General Partnership

Business Tax Identification Number

- Partnership Agreement showing business name and name of partners, and
- Business name filing document, such as Fictitious Name Certificate or Certificate of Trade Name, showing business name and name of partners.

Limited Partnership

Business Tax Identification Number

- Limited Partnership Agreement showing business name and name of partners, and
- Business organizing document filed with and certified by state official, such as Certificate of Limited Partnership, showing business name and name of partners

Limited Liability Partnership

Business Tax Identification Number
Limited Liability Partnership Agreement showing business name and name of partners, and
Business organizing document filed with and certified by state official, such as Certificate of Limited Liability Partnership, showing business name and name of partners.

Corporation

Business Tax Identification Number
Articles of Incorporation or Certificate of Incorporation
Corporate Resolution identifying authorized signers if officer names are not listed on Articles of Incorporation or Certificate of Incorporation.

Corporation (Publicly Traded)

Business Tax Identification Number

- Articles of Incorporation or Certificate of Incorporation
- Corporate Resolution identifying authorized signers if officer names are not listed on Articles of Incorporation or Certificate of Incorporation

Professional Corporation

Business Tax Identification Number

- Articles of Incorporation or Certificate of Incorporation
- Corporate Resolution identifying authorized signers if officer names are not listed on Articles of Incorporation or Certificate of Incorporation.

Limited Liability Company

Business Tax Identification Number
- Articles of Organization or Certificate of Formation
- Corporate Resolution identifying authorized signers if officer names are not listed on Articles of Organization or Certificate of Formation

Unincorporated Association

Business Tax Identification Number

- Organizing document, such as Articles of Association (if available)
- You will be prompted to select what type of bank account you prefer to open. Some online banks offer a variety of options, from business economy checking to full analysis business checking.

If you are given the opportunity, select the business debit card option and review all the additional services you can add to your account.

Now that you have opened a business bank account successfully, the next step is establishing a favorable bank rating for your company.

The End.

www.ingramcontent.com/pod-product-compliance
Lightning Source LLC
Chambersburg PA
CBHW021450170526
45164CB00001B/453